THE FALL FESTIVAL

THE FALL FESTIVAL

BY MERCER MAYER

HarperCollinsPublishers

To Tess, Tori, and Tedy Chapell

An Imprint of Sterling Publishing
387 Park Avenue South
New York, NY 10016

A Big Tuna Trading Company, LLC/J. R. Sansevere Book
www.littlecritter.com

ISBN 978-1-4351-4384-5

HarperCollins ISBN: 978-0-06-222992-2

Library of Congress Catalog Card Number: 2008931803

For information about custom editions, special sales,
and premium and corporate purchases, please contact
Sterling Special Sales at 800-805-5489 or specialsales@sterlingpublishing.com.

Manufactured in China

Lot 12 13 SCP 6 5 4 3 2 1

Manufactured 05/2012

It is fall.

The leaves change colors.

They turn yellow and red.

We are driving in the car.

We drive to the Fall Festival.

Lots of critters are there.

We bring a wagon
to hold the things we buy.

I see so many apples.

I try one.

Mom pays the man.

Little Sister has apple cider.

She spills it.

It is sticky.

We go on a hayride.

There is not much hay.

We ride through
a field full of pumpkins.

I watch a critter
shoot pumpkins into the air.
They go SPLAT!

It is fun to watch.

We walk to the apple trees.

I see critters picking apples.

I get to pick apples, too.

Dad buys the apples that we pick.

Mom will make many apple pies.

Yum! I eat another apple.

Mom says, "No more apples."

Next we look for

a Halloween pumpkin.

Some pumpkins are too small.

Some pumpkins
are too funny looking.

I find the perfect pumpkin.

It is big.

Mom finds
the perfect pumpkin, too.
It is not so big.

We play the horseshoe game.

We each get three throws.

We can win prizes.

I go first.

I aim.

I throw.

I fly. Whoops!

I forgot to let go.

Dad goes next.

He wins every time.

He wins a bunny
for Little Sister
and a bear for me.

It is time to go home.

Little Sister pulls the wagon.

I help her.

Dad carries the pumpkin.
Mom picks up the apples
that we drop.

I think fall is great,
but I ate too many apples.

The End.

LION & TIGER & BEAR

Tag! You're It!

Ethan Long

ABRAMS BOOKS FOR YOUNG READERS · NEW YORK

TO MY FAMILY & FRIENDS.
ALL OF THEM.

The artwork in this book was created digitally in Adobe Photoshop using its array of brushes, which include but are not limited to: the fuzzy brush, the airbrush, the brush that looks like chalk, and my savior, the eraser brush, which fixed all of my painting mishaps.

Library of Congress Cataloging-in-Publication Data
Long, Ethan, author, illustrator.
Lion & Tiger & Bear in Tag! You're it! / Ethan Long.
pages cm
Summary: Tiger and Bear try to entice Lion to stop painting his masterpiece and play a game of tag instead.
ISBN 978-1-4197-1896-0 (hardcover)
[1. Lion—Fiction. 2. Tiger—Fiction. 3. Bears—Fiction. 4. Tag games—Fiction. 5. Play—Fiction.
6. Friendship—Fiction.] I. Title. II. Title: Lion and Tiger and Bear in Tag! You're it! III. Title: Tag! You're it!
PZ7.L8453Li 2016
[E]—dc23
2015013076

Printed and bound in China
10 9 8 7 6 5 4 3 2 1

Abrams Books for Young Readers are available at special discounts when purchased in quantity for premiums and promotions as well as fundraising or educational use. Special editions can also be created to specification. For details, contact specialsales@abramsbooks.com or the address below.

THE ART OF BOOKS SINCE 1949
115 West 18th Street
New York, NY 10011
www.abramsbooks.com

This is Lion.

This is Tiger.

This is Bear.

They are good friends.

It was a beautiful morning in Green Hills Hollow.
Lion was enjoying some time in his Alone Spot when
suddenly . . .

Lion started painting again, but then . . .

And with that . . .

Lion made himself extremely unavailable.

But tag was a little boring with just the two of them.

So they decided to spice things up.

Lion was going to finish his painting, even if it took him all day.

So he decided to go to the place
where Tiger and Bear would
never follow him . . .

THE DEEP, DARK WOODS!
HOO! HOO!
CHICKA CHICKA CHICKA
CLICK CLICK CLICK
CLICK CLICK
CROAK CROAK CROAK

So Lion dipped . . .

and dabbed.

He splotched . . .

and swooshed.

Until he had created a masterpiece!

Lion and Tiger and Bear gazed at the painting for a long time.

Until . . .

It was playtime once again.